Children of the Sun

The Pueblos, Navajos, and Apaches of New Mexico

by MAUDIE ROBINSON

Illustrated with photographs

Julian Messner New York

Children of the Sun

The Pueblos, Navajos, and Apaches of New Mexico

Published by Julian Messner, a Division of Simon & Schuster, Inc.
1 West 39 Street, New York, N. Y. 10018. All rights reserved.

Printed in the United States of America

Design by Marjorie Zaum

Poem on page 85 from *Diné Baa-Hane* of Fort Defiance, Navajo Nation, a voice of the Indian people, and *El Grito del Norte* of Espanola, New Mexico. Reprinted with their kind permission.

Library of Congress Cataloging in Publication Data

Robinson, Maudie.
   Children of the sun: The Pueblos, Navajos and Apaches of New Mexico

   SUMMARY: Discusses the history, tribal customs, arts, and way of life of New Mexico's Pueblo, Navajo, and Apache Indians.
   1. Pueblo Indians—Juvenile literature. 2. Navajo Indians—Juvenile literature. 3. Apache Indians—Juvenile literature. [1. Pueblo Indians. 2. Navajo Indians. 3. Apache Indians] I. Title.
E99.P9R56   970.4'89   73-736
ISBN 0-671-32596-5 (lib. bdg.)

For Kathy, Steven, and Polly

ACKNOWLEDGMENT

I wish to thank Anthony Purley, Director of the American Indian Culture Center of the University of California at Los Angeles, for reading my book and offering many helpful suggestions. Also, Frank Anaya of the New Mexico Department of Development for his untiring efforts in helping me in my search for photographs of ancient handicrafts; Barbara Sena, for her interest and help in securing important statistics from the State Department of Indian Education; Eileen Eshner, head of the Carnegie Library, Las Vegas, New Mexico, for her continual help in ferreting out and ordering books and pamphlets from other libraries for me.

My special thanks must go to my good friend, Ray Moquino, who brought his family to visit me and kindly invited me to his village of Santo Domingo to view the sacred dances of his people.

I gratefully acknowledge the help and patient instruction of my editor, Lee Hoffman, and her assistant, Elaine Landau, and the neverfailing encouragement of my friend and literary agent, Edith Margolis.

Maudie Robinson

CONTENTS

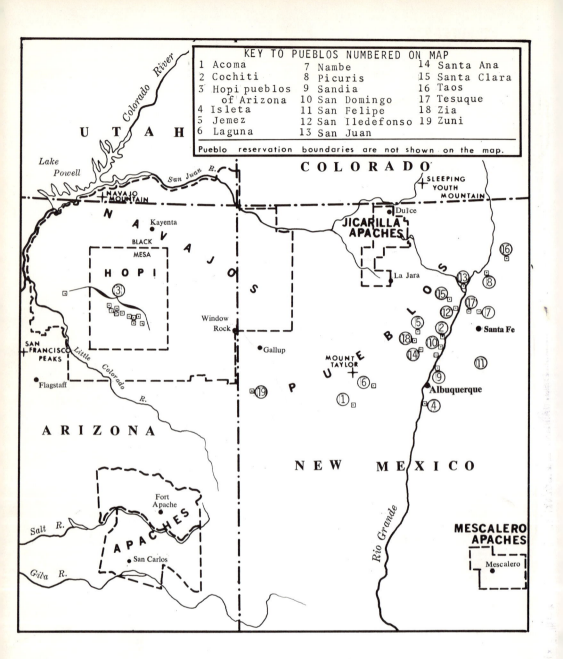

KEY TO PUEBLOS NUMBERED ON MAP

1 Acoma	7 Nambe	14 Santa Ana
2 Cochiti	8 Picuris	15 Santa Clara
3 Hopi pueblos	9 Sandia	16 Taos
of Arizona	10 San Domingo	17 Tesuque
4 Isleta	11 San Felipe	18 Zia
5 Jemez	12 San Iledefonso	19 Zuni
6 Laguna	13 San Juan	

Pueblo reservation boundaries are not shown on the map.

Chapter 1

THE FIRST AMERICANS IN NEW MEXICO

Today, about 70,000 Native Americans live in their own villages in the western half of New Mexico. They, along with other Native Americans throughout the country, believe that the sun is the "Life Giver" to all people and living things. That is why they sometimes call themselves "Children of the Sun".

The Children of the Sun are divided into many groups, three of which live in New Mexico. They are the Pueblos, the Navajos, and the Apaches.

The Pueblos were probably the first of these groups to settle in the Southwest many thousands of years ago. At first, they were wandering hunters and seed gatherers, living on whatever plants and animals they found. But once they learned to plant corn, they settled down as farmers and raised crops of corn, beans, and squash. They built houses of stone and clay, made baskets and pottery, and learned to weave cotton into cloth.

The Navajos and Apaches, who were warriors and hunters, arrived in the Southwest less than a thousand years ago. When the hunting was poor, and they were hungry, they raided the peaceful Pueblo farming villages and stole their food.

The Spanish explorers, who came to the Southwest from Mexico about 1540, found these Indian people and called them by Spanish names: Navajo and Apache for the hunters, Pueblo for the village farmers. *Pueblo* is the Spanish word for village. The Indians have kept these names until today.

The first explorers were followed, fifty years later, by Spanish and Mexican settlers who brought with them animals and plants that were new to the Indians. Cattle, horses, sheep, and goats were useful to the Indians. Wheat, alfalfa, fruit trees, and other plants were also welcome.

But Spanish rule meant other, unwelcome changes in Indian life. The Pueblos were allowed to keep the lands where they had lived for generations, but they were ordered to become Christians. The Indian religions were forbidden under pain of death. Many of them were forced to serve their Spanish conquerors in menial jobs.

In 1680, the Pueblos joined together in revolt against the Spaniards and drove them from their territory. But twelve years later, the Spaniards once more came to rule the Pueblo Indians. When at last the people rebuilt their towns, they locked away the years of war and never, as a people, returned to them. But neither did they submit.

When Mexico won its independence from Spain in

1821, the Southwest came under Mexican rule. About this time, immigrants from Europe as well as from the United States poured into this territory. But soon afterward, the United States and Mexico went to war against each other. When it was over, Mexico which was defeated, ceded to the United States much of the Southwest. This area included what are now the states of Arizona, New Mexico, California, and Texas.

The coming of the American settlers greatly changed the Southwest. The population grew quickly, and ranchers claimed lands that had been used by Indians for centuries. Too many animals were allowed to graze, and the grass and plants were eaten, leaving the soil bare. Trees

The inside of this 1883 Pueblo house looks very much like the adobe dwelling of today's Pueblo Indians. The pottery, corn, and strings of dried chili peppers that decorate the room are still a vital part of their life and culture.

were cut down for timber. Settlers seized control of water wherever they could, and Indian lands suffered. The tribes banded together and fought to prevent the white man's expansion.

However, after years of struggle, the whites won. In 1863, the United States government assigned all Pueblo Indians certain lands called reservations. It also promised the Pueblo Indians that the land would be theirs "as long as the grass shall grow and the rivers run." President Abraham Lincoln gave a silver cane as a symbol of peace to each tribal chief. He also assured them that the government would keep its promise. But the promise was never kept!

The Navajos did not live in towns or villages. They lived in small family groups, tending their horses, sheep, and goats and raising corn, vegetables, and fruit wherever they could find water enough for crops. From time to time, they raided ranches to try to stop the white man from stealing their land and mistreating their people. When the settlers protested, the government sent in troops to put down the Indians.

The soldiers killed many Navajos, destroyed their crops, and burned their homes and orchards. Then they rounded up about eight thousand Navajo men, women, and children and marched them to Fort Sumner, in eastern New Mexico. A great number of them died on "The Long

Walk." The Navajos who survived were imprisoned at Fort Sumner for four years. There, many of them died from starvation and disease.

The remaining Navajos were finally defeated and signed a peace treaty with the United States. By the terms of that treaty, they agreed to live on lands reserved for them in northwestern New Mexico, northeastern Arizona, and southeastern Utah.

The Navajo reservation was in the least desirable sections of the country. Much of the land was desert and had very little water. White hunters had killed or driven away from surrounding areas much of the large game animals that in the past had provided food and clothing for the Indians.

After many years of wandering through their reservation lands, the Navajos settled down and built their homes in western New Mexico and northeastern Arizona. They began to farm and raise sheep like the Pueblos, but still continued to fight against both Indians and white people who took their land.

The Apaches saw the government in Washington continue to break treaties with the Navajos and Pueblos. This made them even more determined not to give up their land or freedom, and they fought on for another twenty years.

The United States Army killed large numbers of them

Geronimo was an outstanding Apache leader who valiantly fought for his people against the white man. This photograph, taken in September, 1886, shows Geronimo (front row, fourth from left) and his devoted followers on their way to Fort Sam Houston, Texas, guarded by Army troops.

and imprisoned many of their leaders. The Apaches finally surrendered and in 1887 signed a peace treaty with the United States. Some of them were sent to live on reservations in northern and southern New Mexico and others to Arizona, Oklahoma, and Florida.

Meanwhile, to help all the Native Americans, the federal government had set up the Bureau of Indian Affairs. But right from the start, the Bureau was faced with many problems. The Children of the Sun were given land which was so poor that it could not be used for farming. In addition, the government agents did not understand the Indian people and their way of life, and often did not do the right things to help them.

During the years that followed, the Apaches, Navajos, and Pueblos lived in poverty and sickness, with bitter memories of their treatment. After years of broken promises and mistreatment by Washington, they no longer trusted the white man.

The churches and the government wanted to make the Native Americans like the white man. The churches had already started schools for many Indian children. So, following their example in the 1930's, the government set up boarding schools for all Indian children.

But the parents did not want their children to attend the boarding schools, which were far away from their homes. This meant they could see their children only

In 1886, these Apache young people were taken from their reservation and brought to the Indian school at Carlisle, Pennsylvania, to be educated. However, to the white man, Indian education meant more than just teaching him to read and write English—it meant destroying his pride and tribal culture as well. In trying to make these Apaches look like the white man, school officials cut their hair, took away their tribal clothes and forbid them to use their own language.

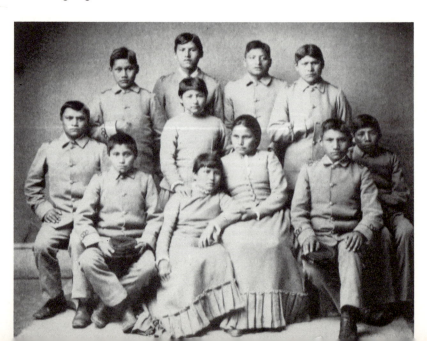

twice a year. Besides, white teachers in these schools were trying to destroy tribal ways and customs. They called the Native American children heathens, and forced them to give up their sacred tribal religions for Christianity. In addition, they made the children wear white man's clothing and punished them for even speaking their own native language.

Often the children ran away from school and traveled alone for many miles to return to their reservations. Once they were home, their tribe hid them from the school authorities, who came after the children to take them back to boarding school.

In 1924, the federal government passed a law giving full citizenship to all Native Americans. However, since New Mexico and some other states did not recognize the law, Indians were not allowed to vote, own property, or attend public schools. It was not until 1934 that New Mexico granted the rights of citizenship to the Indian people living in that state.

But the lives of the Indian children did not really begin to change until 1945. Then their brothers and sisters, who had served all over the world in the Armed Forces during World War II, came home with a new awareness of the outside world.

They said: "Out there in the white man's world, things are different. Some things seem better. But we are poor, and do not have their advantages. Some of the old ways are not working, so we must learn some of the new ways. We must learn paper."

"Learning paper" was their way of saying learning to read and write English. Some felt this was important if their people were to have a better life. As these young men began taking part in tribal councils, their influence spread. Slowly, others began to accept their new way of thinking.

Today, some young Indians are learning English so that they can compete in the white man's world. They know that if they learn English they will be able to get a better education as well as jobs in nearby cities. Indians are also studying agriculture and new methods of livestock care to improve their soil and herds. They hope these things will provide a better life for their people.

But many of the older Native Americans do not believe these new ways are good. The grandparents have heard stories, told and retold at their firesides, about the white man's cruelty and treachery. They feel that the Indian has nothing to gain by learning to be like the white man. Instead, they want their grandchildren to "walk the Beautiful Way," as their people have always done.

To walk the Beautiful Way, an Indian must be honest and loyal to himself and his tribe. He must be true to his gods and obey the laws of his people. He must treat all

Many Indians feel that each of them must make a choice between living according to his own Indian heritage or leaving it for the white man's world. Others believe the two worlds can be combined, as shown in this picture where an Indian drum is placed alongside graduation pictures.

men as brothers and hold all life sacred.

Many of the young agree with their grandparents, and struggle to preserve their old and precious tribal traditions. But other young people reply that the Children of the Sun can more easily survive and continue to walk the beautiful way if they add the white man's science and knowledge to their own culture.

But how can this be done.?

Can they adopt the white man's ways without losing their own way of life? Will they be happier living this new kind of life? The grandparents say No. Some of the young people say Yes. Others are not certain.

Here is how the Pueblos, Navajos, and Apaches of New Mexico live today.

Chapter 2

THE PEACEFUL PEOPLE

The Pueblo Indians

Nine-year-old Juanito was sitting at his desk waiting impatiently for the school bell to ring. It was almost time to go home, and he was thinking about what he and Antonio, his friend and clan brother, would do after school. They had planned to go to Antonio's home to watch television.

Juanito was looking out the window, not thinking about the lesson, when his teacher called on him to read aloud. He didn't hear her, and had to be asked again. It was difficult for Juanito to read and speak English because it wasn't the language spoken in his village. His people preferred to speak their own traditional dialect, although many of them knew English.

Juanito was disappointed and hurt when his teacher told him that he would have to stay after school until he was able to pay attention in class. She also wanted him to learn to pronounce more English words correctly. He knew the school bus would leave without him, and he would have to walk four miles to get home.

But when his teacher finally dismissed him, Juanito felt better because he found Antonio waiting for him.

As they entered their village, they could smell bread baking in some of the outside ovens. Juanito was born in this Pueblo Indian village, as were his parents and

grandparents. His village looks very much like the other eighteen Pueblo Indian villages in New Mexico, which stretch along the Rio Grande from the city of Taos, near

After a day at school, Pueblo children run down a hill into their village. Pueblo children usually wear the white man's style of clothing to school, but change into traditional Indian clothes when they are at home.

the Colorado border, south to Sante Fe, and southwest to Albuquerque. They continue westward to Gallup, near the Arizona border.

Pueblo Indians are known by the names of their villages. Some of their names are the Taos Indians, the Laguna Indians, and Santa Clara Indians. Juanito is a Santo Domingo Indian. His village is between Santa Fe and Albuquerque.

Some of the Pueblo villages have only two or three hundred people, while others have as many as two thousand. There are about 30,000 Pueblo Indians in all. Since the Pueblo Indians speak four or five different languages, the people of one village often cannot understand the language of another. They speak Tiwa, Tewa, Towa, Keres, and several dialects that are a mixture of two or more of these languages. Most of the young people and many adults can speak with each other only in English. However, the adults usually prefer to speak in the native dialect.

With so many different languages, Pueblo Indians usually have an interesting combination of names. Many of them kept the names that were given to them by the Spaniards, while others have taken English names. It is not unusual for a Pueblo Indian to have two or even three names, as there are names given to them at birth, names given to them by their clan, and sacred names, which are rarely used except on ceremonial occasions.

Each Pueblo village has one or two central plazas, where the public ceremonial dances are performed. The houses face the plaza. Gardens, fields, and pastures stretch out from the villages.

From a distance, Pueblo houses look like rows of mud-colored blocks. They are all made of either sandstone blocks or adobe bricks, plastered together with mud. The sandstone blocks are gathered from the surrounding hills and brought in by horse-drawn wagons or pickup trucks.

The adobe bricks are made by mixing clay, a sticky kind of earth found near the villages, with straw and water. When dried in the sun, they become strong and will last for a very long time. These materials make the houses warm in the winter and cool in the summer.

Some houses are built in tiers three and four stories high. Each tier is smaller than the one on which it rests, so that the houses are shaped something like a pyramid.

Taos Pueblo has kept its fortress-like appearance over the years. In the old days before there were doors and windows in the buildings, the Pueblos would just pull in the ladders from the roof entrance, so their enemies could not enter.

Pueblo women hang strings of dried chili peppers on the adobe walls of their homes until they are ready to use them.

Since there are no stairways, the upper tiers are entered by outdoor ladders.

On the roofs of their dwellings, the women spread their fruits and vegetables to dry. They string chili peppers into scarlet loops and hang them over the outside walls, where the peppers will remain till they are used.

The federal government has installed electric lights and a village water pump in Juanito's village, as well as in several others. But some of the people do not want these things, for they believe the white man's inventions will destroy their old way of life.

They also feel the same way about furniture in their

houses. They sleep on the floor as their ancestors did a hundred years ago, and use a fireplace for cooking and heating. Others, like Juanito's parents, cannot afford furniture.

However, there are some families who own furniture and a television set. These people earn enough money to buy these things by working in nearby towns as nurses, teachers, office workers, carpenters, and janitors.

Juanito's father is a farmer. He uses modern plows, tractors, and harvesters, which are owned by the village but are available to every farmer. He grows corn, alfalfa, beans, potatoes, cabbages, squash, and many other vegetables. When he produces more than his family needs, he sells it. To make extra money in his spare time, he hauls wood for other villagers and the people of the surrounding communities.

After school and on weekends, Juanito helps his father hoe the corn and other vegetables. As they work together, his father tells him how Mother Earth first gave corn to the Pueblo Indians.

Long ago, their people were starving. Mother Earth called for six medicine men, and told each to plant a pebble in the earth. In a few days, six green corn plants were growing where they had placed the pebbles. The Pueblo Indians believe that six different colors of corn—white, blue, red, yellow, purple, and black—grew from these first six plants.

A man chops firewood for his family during the cold winter months. Pueblo Indians live in harmony with nature. While they are alive, they will chop down trees for fuel to warm themselves. But they know that when they die, their bodies will go back into the earth to nourish the trees and other living things.

A Pueblo woman bakes bread as her ancestors did in an ancient outdoor oven called an **horno.** Firewood to fuel the oven is stored on platforms nearby.

Since that time, they have always planted each color in a separate field.

While they work in the fields, father also tells Juanito about living with animals and nature. He teaches him how to make a scarecrow to frighten away the birds who peck at the corn, fruit, and melons. To catch the rabbits that nibble at the young vegetables, they build snares with wire and vines. Father cautions Juanito to watch closely for rattlesnakes, which coil themselves in the shades of the grass and strike without warning.

Some Pueblo girls go to the fields and help hoe and pick the vegetables, but Juanito's sister, Annacita, would rather help her mother at home. She wants to live near her parents when she marries. Now she learns how to keep house in exactly the way her mother and grandmother have always done. She prepares fruits and vegetables for drying on the roof, and pats a fresh coating of mud on the walls of the house to keep them looking smooth and clean.

Annacita watches her mother bake thick loaves of bread in the outside oven, which looks very much like a beehive. Often her mother bakes extra loaves, which she sells in the marketplace in Albuquerque or Santa Fe, along with the pots and jewelry she has made.

At times, Annacita bakes wafer bread. To do this, she heats a flat stone and pours a thin layer of batter on it. When the wafer is done, she peels it off the stone and rolls it up.

31

Her father says that her wafer bread is delicious dipped in stew.

Pueblo Indians eat a great deal of baked bread, usually with the stew they make from their home-grown vegetables. They add beef and mutton when they can afford it. They also enjoy beans, tamales, chili, fruit, and melons.

Pueblo people who remain in their villages usually dress as their ancestors did. Although, like other children, Annacita wears a short cotton dress to school, she takes it off after school and puts on a long skirt like her mother's. And, also like her mother, she will some day wear her hair in bangs across the forehead and tied in back in a bun. When Juanito gets older, he wants to wear his hair tied back in a loop with a string and a headband like his father.

However, there are some Indians who dress like the white man, and wear the latest hair styles. Many of them work in town, where traditional Indian dress and long hair is often frowned on by employers. So they wear work clothes, business suits, uniforms, or whatever the job requires.

Today, most Pueblo children attend public grade schools near their reservation homes, and go to high school in nearby cities. They study the same English textbooks as other children, but find this difficult because English is not their native language. Many become discouraged and leave school.

Now, Pueblo leaders are protesting against the white man's control of the schools. They want to have a voice in what their children study and how their schools are managed. Pueblo Indians live in well organized, peaceful communities where there is little or no juvenile delinquency. They know they could run their own schools as well.

Chapter 3

THE BEAUTIFUL WAY

Pueblo Religion and Customs

When the Spaniards came to the Southwest, they brought priests to convert the Pueblo Indians to the Catholic religion. Later Protestant ministers tried to convert the Indians to their beliefs. Today both Catholic and Protestant churches can be seen near the villages.

The Pueblo Indians feel that the Christian diety is as important as their own diety, "The Great Spirit." So they attend church to worship Jesus Christ. However, after the Christian services are over, the men usually go to their kiva, where the religious clans meet to worship their own gods. They consider the sun, earth, moon, stars, wind, water, lightning, thunder, and all living things as sacred. Each village has two or three kivas, one for each religious clan. Most of the kivas are for men only, but in some villages the women have a kiva of their own. The kiva is a large underground room that contains altars and sacred paintings, much like a church.

Religious instruction for Pueblo Indian boys begin when they are twelve or thirteen years of age. When Juanito is twelve, his father, grandfather, and uncles will decide when

This reservation Catholic church, made of adobe and built in Pueblo style architecture, is a good example of how Spanish and Indian cultures have blended.

The building at the right is a Pueblo kiva.

he will be ready to enter the kiva, and take part in the secret religious ceremonies of his people. There are no written records of these ceremonies, and they will be lost if the young people of each generation do not learn them by heart. Juanito's mother and sister will not be able to see the secret ceremonies, as they are only for the men.

Juanito will learn about his gods and the Beautiful Way. He will find out what the religious signs and symbols mean, as well as how to conduct the secret ceremonies. When he learns the words and songs of a ceremony, he will greatly honor his family. His father will announce this good news to the whole village, and his relatives will prepare a feast to celebrate the occasion. All the guests will bring Juanito gifts, and congratulate his family.

Annacita does not take instruction in the kiva, but she takes part in the ceremonial dances held in the village square. Both boys and girls are taught these dances when they are only two and three years old. Dressed in ceremonial clothing, they dance in perfect rhythm alongside their parents. Most of the time, there are two groups of dancers. One group dances while the other group rests, so the dancing continues all day.

Each dance, which has its own name—Corn Dance, Snake Dance, Deer Dance, Buffalo Dance—is a result of worship in the kiva. The dancers may be praying for rain or for a successful hunt. Sometimes they give thanks for everyone's

Many Pueblo dances have a special religious meaning. Here Pueblo Indians, dressed in ceremonial clothing, perform the Deer Dance.

good health and good fortune. In the Corn Dance, for example, the dancers re-enact the planting, growing, and harvesting of the corn.

Corn is used in almost every Pueblo ceremonial. A bowl of sacred cornmeal is placed on the altar of the kiva. The Pueblos sing to their gods, hoping the gods will be pleased and ripen their corn. One song goes like this:

Come lovely cloud!
Come closer!
Bring the rain!
The corn ears are waiting!
Ah, the rain god hears!
The cloud grows black!
It is moving!
It brings rain to the little corn ears!

Pueblo Indians believe that disease and misfortune are sometimes caused by evil spirits in the body of a person or animal. If that person chokes or is strangled, an evil spirit is trying to get into his body. They call a medicine man to drive away the spirit. The medicine man is part of their ancient heritage and culture, and he performs the same rites today as he did years ago.

Annacita and Juanito are taught to respect blind, deaf, and crippled people. Pueblo Indians feel that they are special people who are dear to their gods, and that misfortune will come to anyone who laughs at them.

Juanito and Annacita believe that if they obey the rules of their people and worship their gods, they will be able to walk the Beautiful Way all of their lives.

Chapter 4

CRIMSON JUGS AND SILVER BRACELETS

Pueblo Arts and Crafts

Before Columbus discovered America in 1492, Pueblo Indians were making jewelry from bear claws, eagle beaks, bones, and seeds which they found near their homes. Later they made bracelets and rings out of silver coins the Spaniards brought with them. Today, the Pueblos still make jewelry, but now they buy silver bars from jewelry dealers.

Indian jewelry is often studded with obsidian and turquoise. Obsidian is a black stone found near lava beds in western New Mexico. Turquoise is mined in New Mexico and is sacred to the Indians.

An ancient legend says that a strange, beautiful maiden was once seen among the Indian villages. She had long blue-black hair that hung below her waist. One day, while walking with the village girls, she sank into a deep hole in the earth. Only her blue-black hair remained above the ground. The next morning, a large stone as bright as the sky stood where the maiden's hair had been. Some of the villagers said, "The stone is blue." Others said, "The stone is green." But their medicine man said, "It is both. It is blue-green and and shall be called turquoise. The beautiful maiden was a spirit person whom Mother Earth sent to bring us the turquoise. It shall be our sacred stone."

Besides jewelry, Pueblo men make serving trays, jewelry boxes, belts, buttons, ash trays, and many other items. Juanito is too impatient to do such tedious work, but he likes to watch his grandfather create beautiful bracelets and rings from a bar of silver. Like other Pueblo men, his grandfather still uses the old tools in his work, which have been handed down from generation to generation. He makes his own forge, anvil, and chisels, but he buys his scissors, tongs, pliers, and awls.

Although many of the designs are old, today's silversmiths are also creating new designs and different articles for sale. The Zuni make silver jewelry inlaid with different-colored stones in ancient designs. Silversmiths are usually men, but some women are now doing this work too.

Some Pueblo men also make kachina dolls. These are brightly painted dolls of wood that the Pueblo tribes use in their religious ceremonies.

Many Pueblo women make pottery. To dig for clay, Annacita and her mother go to the same clay pit their ancestors went to. Before taking the clay, they say, "Thank you, Mother Earth, for your clay. Guide our fingers as we make this into beautiful pots."

Annacita watches her mother closely as she shapes her pot. She starts with the bottom of the pot, patting the wet clay until it is round and flat. Next she forms a clay rope,

Zuni silversmiths are skilled artists. They design the silver frame into which they will carefully set small pieces of polished rust, black, white and turquoise stones. The ancient designs on these handmade jewelry pieces tell about Zuni culture as well as beautify their wearers.

Expert potter Maria Martinez of San Ildefonso Pueblo spent long hours studying the designs on ancient Pueblo pottery, which she then used in her own work. In doing so, she once again brought to life and made popular this ancient art of her people. Today, examples of Ms. Martinez' pottery can be found in every major museum in the United States as well as in Europe.

coiling it, one row on top of the other, until the pot is as high as she wishes it to be. Then she dips her fingers in water and smooths the pot. When the pot is dry, she polishes it inside and out with small stones until it has a smooth surface and is ready to paint.

Boiling and mixing dyes to paint the pottery takes the hand of an expert. Carefully Mother drops dried leaves, berries, roots, and a ground-up pebble in the pot of boiling water to get the proper color. She strains the dye through a cloth and sets it aside to cool. Then she starts all over again making another color.

After the pot is painted, it must be baked over a slow fire for several hours to make it strong and leakproof. It can then be used for cooking or decoration.

The women of each pueblo make distinctively different pots. Santo Domingo women make a beautiful rusty red pot with a pale-blue and creamy-white design. The Jémez pueblo women use a tan background with designs of brilliant reds and greens. From the San Ildefonso and Santa Clara women come a highly prized pot that is as black as night and has a luminous sheen.

Indians are now finding a wide market for their products. However, considering the amount of talent and effort that goes into each individually crafted article, the Indian does not receive enough money for his work.

Nevertheless, Pueblo Indians are encouraging their chil-

dren to learn the ancient crafts and arts. Talented young Indians attend the Institute of American Indian Arts at Santa Fe, which is a combined academic high school and art institute. As they study their people's history and art, they realize that the beautiful jewelry and pottery they make keep their ancient culture alive.

Today, Indian students keep alive their peoples' art and culture through their own work. This painting was done by a student at the Institute of American Indian Arts.

Chapter 5

WE ARE THE PEOPLE

The Navajos

Ason-ne opened her eyes and looked to the east through the open door of the hogan. As ribbons of sunlight streamed in, she realized that she was late. Dressing quickly, she rushed through the open door and began to run toward the rising sun. Her brother, Keedah, followed, running a few feet behind her, as it would be improper for him to be in front of his sister. Ason-ne runs every morning, for her people believe this will give her good health and beauty.

Ason-ne and Keedah are Navajo Indians. There are more than 120,000 people in their tribe, which is the largest in the United States. The Navajo reservation begins in New Mexico and stretches across Arizona into southern Utah.

Deserts, rock canyons, rugged mountains, rolling prairies, and highlands are all part of the Navajo landscape. In summer, the sun scorches the earth; in winter, the snow falls for weeks at a time. But despite the burning heat and bitter cold, the Navajos do not want to leave their land. To them, it is a wild and beautiful place where the wind whistles and sings across the prairies.

The sun sprays their four sacred mountains with as many colors as the Navajo woman weaves into her rug. They believe that holy persons, or spirits, live in these mountains and watch over the Navajo people.

For hundreds of years, the many small bands of Navajos thought of themselves as one great body of people who shared a common language and way of life. They called themselves "The People." Only recently have they considered themselves a tribe. That is because they have joined together in council meetings to find ways of helping all Navajos.

Ason-ne and Keedah have typical Navajo names. Ason-ne means "tall girl," and Keedah is similar to the American name Sonny. Ason-ne and Keedah also have sacred Navajo names, known only to their family.

At school, they are called Mary Kay Nabahe and Keedah John Nabahe. Usually the father's first name is used for the family last name, and government or school officials add non-Indian first names. Since their father's name is Nabahe Begay, Ason-ne and Keedah's last name is Nabahe. Nabahe means "fighting man."

Like most Navajos, Ason-ne and Keedah live in a hogan, which is rounded at the top and has eight sides and a roof made of logs sealed together with mud. Often grass grows on the mud roof and makes the hogan look very much like the earth and trees surrounding it. In fact, a stranger may pass by without noticing that a hogan is there.

Inside, the hogan has one large room, with a hard-packed earth floor. The walls are unplastered, and the spaces be-

One out of every four Navajo families live in a hogan like the one in front of which this man in standing. When a man marries, he usually builds a hogan near his wife's family. Property, including the hogan and grazing lands, is owned by the wife and is passed on to the children through her.

tween the logs are used for storing things. The hogan has one door, which always faces east because the sun rises there. Blankets usually cover the doors but, today, some hogans have store-bought windows and doors. In the center of the room is a wood stove. Navajos sleep on the floor with their feet pointed toward the stove. They believe that sleeping in a circle will keep evil spirits away during the night.

By the time Ason-ne and Keedah return from their morning run, their mother is preparing a breakfast of round flat cakes fried in hot deep fat. These cakes, which are a favorite Navajo dish, are called fried bread. Ason-ne measures coffee into a big pot of boiling water. When their father returns from rounding up the horses that run loose on the prairie, the family sits down on a rug to eat breakfast. During the meal, Grandmother never looks directly at her son-in-law, for the Navajos believe that it is bad luck for a man to look in the eyes of his mother-in-law.

Mrs. Nabahe and Grandmother have brushed their shining black hair and looped it into buns on the back of their heads. Both of them are wearing long full cotton skirts. Grandmother's blouse is purple, and Mrs. Nabahe's blouse is dark red. Mrs. Nabahe also wears a silver necklace that her husband made. He designed it with dangles shaped like squash blossoms.

Keedah is wearing levis and a cotton shirt, Ason-ne is wearing a short cotton dress. Most Navajo children wear the white man's style of clothes to school.

Ason-ne and Keedah are surprised and pleased when their mother stirs sugar into their coffee, for there hasn't been any sugar for several days. Mrs. Nabahe explains that their father traded a sheepskin for the sugar at the trading post the day before.

After breakfast, Nabahe puts on his broad-brimmed western hat and leaves in his wagon to haul water for the family. He and other Navajo men wish there were deep water wells near their homes. With water for irrigating, they could grow more vegetables, have larger cornfields, and raise more sheep. Some of the food and sheep might even be sold to buy clothing and other things. Then they would not have to leave the reservation to find jobs in the outside world. Mr. Nabahe sometimes finds a few days of ranch work, or joins the firefighters when the national forests are on fire.

Ason-ne and Keedah go to the brush corral and let out their herd of sheep and goats. While they tend the animals, Keedah sings a song to the herd. Ason-ne joins in when she knows a song. Singing is an important part of Navajo life, and they know many kinds of songs. They believe that certain songs will keep the animals safe from coyotes and poisonous foods.

Before me peaceful,
Behind me peaceful,
My sheep are peaceful all around me.
I hear the peaceful voice of my sheep.
No harm will come to them.
My sheep will walk in peace.

Ason-ne is eleven years old and Keedah is ten, but both have been herding sheep since they were six or seven. They know their sheep by name, and can pick them out from other flocks. They stay on the prairie with the sheep until sunset.

Sometimes their Mother gives them cold fried bread for their lunch. She has also taught them where to find food on the prairie when they are hungry. They know how to pick cactus fruit without pricking their fingers, and where to dig for camotes, which they sometimes call wild potatoes. They know how to trap a rabbit and roast it over a small fire.

They are also used to going for many hours without food. Their grandmother tells them this is good, for when an evil spirit visits the hogan bringing cold and hunger, they will be able to endure with strength and patience. But today, they are thinking of the roasted meat and rich stew they will eat when they return home.

When Mother and Grandmother butcher a sheep, they

Young Navajos graze their sheep in a beautiful natural setting that is typical of Navajo country. Navajos love the raw and rugged beauty of the giant sandstone formations that bathe in sunlight throughout the day and stand majestically against a star-filled sky at night.

waste nothing. They cut the sheepskin away from the meat, scrape the inside, and stretch the skin on the ground to dry. They empty and wash all the inside parts and pour the waste material on their garden for fertilizer. They clean the head and feet and put them in the stew pot with the heart, liver, kidneys, and other parts. They crack the bones and extract the marrow, which also goes into the stew. For seasoning, they add herbs and dried chili peppers. The stew will simmer slowly on a small fire during the day. Later in the summer, they will have squash, green corn, and beans, which they grow, to add to the stew pot.

Mother always dries some of the meat to use in the future. She slices the meat into thin strips and hangs them on the drying racks that stand near the hogan. After having been dried in the sun, this meat will keep for months. This dried meat is called charqui, or jerky. Ason-ne and Keedah like to chew the jerky, and Father likes the strips soaked and cooked with vegetables.

Ason-ne and Keedah live deep inside the Navajo reservation, where there are hardly any white people. In fact, their teacher at the reservation school and the merchant at the trading post are the only white persons they know.

The trading post is a store where the family trade their rugs, jewelry, and sheep for food and clothing. But it is much more than a store. It is also the post office, employment agency, local bank, and social center for the Navajo

At a trading post on their reservation, Navajos exchange their hand-made rugs for food and supplies.

people on the reservation. In the last few years, some of the trading posts have added motels, restaurants, and museums for tourists.

Many Navajo families depend on the white merchant for a number of things. He advises them in legal matters, fills out their government forms, and sometimes finds employment for them. However, most tribe members feel that Navajos should own and run their own trading posts, so that all profit from Indian products goes back to Indians. A few Navajos now do have their own trading posts, and more of them hope to in the future.

The Navajos who live on the borders of the reservation have a different life, for they are near good highways and shopping centers, and can easily travel to their jobs in nearby cities. Since they work in the white man's world, many of them adopted the white man's ways of living. They live in modern houses and dress in the current white fashions. They own cars and television sets, and their children play baseball and go to the movies.

Ason-ne and Keedah have never looked at television. In fact, the only movies they have seen have been old ones shown at their school.

Most Navajo children who live far back in the reservation, away from the modern world, have never seen these things. But they prefer to live where they do, and enjoy their own way of life. When Navajo children are sent to boarding schools in the cities, they have a difficult time getting used to the white man's customs. As a result, many of them leave school and return to their reservations.

Many Indians have become angered by what the white man teaches white as well as Indian children about the Native Americans. The Indians say that when a white man fights for the freedom of his people, he is called a hero, but when an Indian fights for his people, he is called a bloodthirsty savage. They point to history books that show Indians as warlike and uncivilized. Yet when Columbus discovered America, many tribes were living peaceably in well-organized villages. They were enjoying freedom.

"Even our name is the mistake of the white man," declared one angry young Indian. "When Columbus discovered America, he thought he had discovered India, so we have been called Indians ever since."

Navajo people want their children to learn, but they want schools on the reservation itself that are run by Navajos. They believe these schools must teach their children to take pride in their ancient language, culture, and heritage. For Navajos feel only this will preserve their old and precious way of life. To carry through this idea, the Navajos have started the Ramah High School. This bilingual reservation school (both Navajo and English are spoken) has an almost zero drop-out rate. It is run by a highly active five-member Indian school board. The Navajos also have their own community college.

Navajos have their own tribal government, headed by a tribal chairman who is chosen by the people. They have a main tribal council, which is made up of representatives of community chapters. The community council tries to solve family disputes and determines homesites, grazing permits, and water rights. If the problem cannot be solved, it is then submitted to the main tribal council. The many community chapters are necessary, since the Navajos have the largest reservation, with people living in two states. However, since most of their land is in Arizona, with just a small amount in New Mexico, their tribal headquarters are in Window Rock, Arizona.

Chapter 6

SONGS AND
SAND PAINTINGS

Navajo Religion and Customs

Navajos call the earth Changing Woman, for she changes with the seasons. Grandmother often tells Ason-ne and Keedah about Changing Woman's son.

Long, long ago, evil monsters who lived on the earth ate Navajo children. Soon there would not have been any Navajos left, for their children could not grow up to have other children. Then Changing Woman gave birth to a son.

She hid him from the monsters until he was a young man. All during the time she cared for him, Changing Woman taught her son to love his people and their precious tribal ways. The noble young man became determined to free his people, and decided to ask his father's help. To do so, he traveled on a rainbow up to the house of Sun, the Life Giver (his father), who gave him a magic bow and arrows.

When the son came back to earth, he slew the evil monsters. Changing Woman named him Monster Slayer. Now the Navajo children could grow up and have children of their own. They grew to be a large tribe, and today Navajos worship Monster Slayer with ceremonies and dances.

Navajos feel that their lives are affected by good and evil spirits. Ason-ne and Keedah are taught many ways to please the spirits. When planting corn, they add a few grains for the bird and insect spirits, and they sing:

Four for the cutworm,
Four for the crow,
Four for the beetle,
And four to grow.

To the Navajo, the wind has secret power. So Ason-ne and Keedah call it by its secret name, asking it to let the corn prosper. When the corn is stored for winter, they place a stalk having two good ears in the storage pit to ensure a good crop the following year.

Navajos never touch a tree struck by lighting, for lightning is a spirit that must be respected. Neither will they kill snakes, for the evil spirits in snakes can bring evil to their hogans.

Navajo religious ceremonies are called Sings, and their medicine men are called Singers. Singers learn the chants of the different sings. Some of these are the Blessing Way Chant for curing common diseases, Feather Way for headaches, Bead Way for skin diseases, and Big Star Way for bad dreams.

In the Blessing Way Chant, the Singer chants and performs ancient rites for several hours in the sick person's

At an exhibit for visitors, two Navajo medicine men show how to create a sandpainting. The Navajo religion has at least 35 different rituals, but because each ritual is so complex, no one medicine man knows them all.

hogan. By sifting different colors of sand through his fingers, the Singer makes a sand painting on the hogan floor. This is to identify the cause of the illness, and drive away any evil spirits that may be present. Then, while the Singer chants, the sick person is carefully laid on the sand painting to be near his gods. Relatives and friends of the patient fast during the chant, drinking only an herb medicine to cleanse their bodies. The singer tells them to think good thoughts, so that good spirits will visit the hogan.

After the ceremony, the sand painting is destroyed, and

the sand is thrown in four directions. In this way, the evil spirits will be confused, and the contents of the painting cannot be used against others living in the hogan.

Navajo healers have been successful in many cases where doctors have failed. In fact, in 1969, the National Institute of Mental Health began a program that pays six Navajo medicine men to teach twelve young Indians the elaborate ceremonies that often cure mental illness among their people.

A group of young Navajo chanters.

Each medicine man has two students who meet with him nightly to learn the rituals, songs, and sand paintings. It takes a full year to learn a single chant.

The Navajo medicine man is very important to his people. He represents a vital part of Navajo life and religion.

Chapter 7

SILVER JEWELRY
AND STORYTELLING RUGS

Navajo Arts and Crafts

Ason-ne sits on the ground carding wool as her mother carefully weaves a red zigzig line into a rug. This jagged line is lightning. There are also black clouds in the rug, for Mrs. Nabahe is weaving a picture of a thunderstorm. She works carefully, for a mistake would make her rug imperfect, and she would be ashamed to offer it for sale.

But before she can weave her rug, Mrs. Nabahe must wash, card, and spin the wool into thread. Carding is like combing, but it is much harder to do because the wool is very thick. The wool must be carded for hours with a carding comb, a flat board covered with a piece of leather containing wire teeth.

To spin the wool into thread, Mrs. Nabahe uses a small spinning wheel, which she supports with her knees and twirls with her fingers. This, too, is tiring work, so sometimes the Grandmother spins while she rests.

After the thread is spun, it is ready for dyeing. Mrs. Nabahe makes her dyes from dried plants, bark, roots, and berries. Each color has a meaning. Red is the color of lightning, while yellow is the sun's glow. Black is for joy and

63

A Navajo woman prepares to weave fleece from the sheep in her flock. For generations, the Navajo have tended sheep which have provided the tribe with food and clothing as well as warmth and wealth from traditional rugs and blankets.

hope, for the precious rain clouds are black. A jagged line stands for lightning, a wavy line for water or rain, stripes for the sun's rays, and a cross for the morning star. Mrs. Nabahe must always leave a break somewhere in her pattern, usually around the border. Navajos believe that a woman's spirit may be trapped inside the rug and cause her death or injury.

Navajos learned weaving from the Pueblo Indians. In the old days, during their raids on Pueblo villages, Navajos carried away the women. While they were captives, these

Pueblo women taught the Navajo women to weave. Mrs. Nabahe still uses the ancient Pueblo loom to weave her rug. This loom is made of poles, ropes, and stones, and stands upright near the hogan. Mrs. Nabahe sits on the ground, her back very straight, and patiently weaves for long hours at a time.

Navajo rugs are known and prized everywhere. Besides being works of art, they are strong and durable. In Southwestern homes, they are used as floor and wall coverings, drapes, bedspreads, couch covers, and car robes.

Each Navajo rug is priced according to its size and work-

Navajo women weave nature patterns into their rugs as they sit outdoors at their handmade wooden looms.

Each Navajo rug is a work of art, and Navajo women take pride in their perfection. However, each woman makes sure to weave a tiny mistake, usually so small it cannot be seen, into her rug. She does this because Navajos believe perfection is a quality only for the gods.

manship. Today, they are so highly esteemed that their prices have skyrocketed. If Mrs. Nabahe's rug is tightly woven in a sharp, clear design, she may receive as much as two or three hundred dollars for a six-by-nine feet rug. A few years ago, she would have received only twenty or thirty dollars for the same rug. However, the merchant who buys it from her may sell it for more than six hundred or even a thousand dollars. Of course, this is unfair to Mrs. Nabahe, who should get a fairer share of the profits, for she is still receiving only a few cents an hour for her labor.

The price of Indian jewelry has also zoomed on today's market. For this reason, some Navajo men are becoming full-time silversmiths. They hope to be able to make a living without leaving the reservation during the long winter months. However, stores have been flooded with machine-made turquoise and silver jewelry decorated with Indian designs. People are buying jewelry in the false belief that it is handmade by the Indians. This is discouraging more Navajo men from returning to their old craft of silversmithing.

The Navajos learned silversmithing from the Spanish. Keedah's father creates his own jewelry designs, using the old-fashioned Pueblo forge and tools. Keedah is learning to make beautiful designs also. Once Father helped him to make a bracelet, and now Ason-ne proudly wears it.

In the future, the Navajos hope to make more money on their handmade crafts. They want to set up their own

shops, where their rugs, jewelry, and other items can be sold directly to the public. This way, the Navajos will receive all the profits, and they will be able to make a living from their crafts.

Recently the Navajo Tribal Council set up an arts-and-crafts market where the individual Navajos can sell their products for a good price. Similar markets are being planned throughout the reservation.

Ms. Alice Begay prepares a fabric to be tie-dyed. She and her daughter head the Red Rock Tie-Dyeing Corporation, a business on the Navajo reservation. Their tie-dyed products have not only captured the interest of local buyers, but also of East Coast fabric buyers and fashion magazine editors.

Chapter 8

THE LAST WARRIORS

Apache Indians

Jerry is an eleven-year-old Apache Indian. His real name is Geronimo. He was named after the famous Apache warrior Geronimo, who led his people in their last great fight for freedom against the United States Army. Jerry's last name is Vicente. Some Apaches have taken Spanish last names, while others have kept their Apache names.

Today two tribes of Apaches live on reservations in New Mexico. The Jicarilla Apaches live in the northern part of the state, near the town of Dulce, while the Mescalero Apaches live in southern New Mexico, near the city of Alamogordo. Although there are under four thousand people in both tribes, their reservations cover more than a million acres of land.

Jerry belongs to the Jicarilla tribe, but he also feels close to the Mescalero Apache. They speak the same language, and their religion and customs are somewhat the same. At times, they attend each other's religious ceremonies.

Most Apache homes are surrounded by wide grasslands, high mountains, and streams of clear, cold water. Jerry sees wild turkeys nesting in the juniper and pine trees, as well as deer, elk, and antelope running through the forests.

Before there were reservations, the Apache lived in dome-shaped dwellings of poles and brush called wicki-ups. A wickiup had a central fireplace with a vent hole above it through which the smoke escaped. Because Apaches were wanderers, they had few possessions. They left their wickiups standing and built others wherever they stopped for a while.

Today, some Apaches live in houses of wood or adobe,

Apache wickiups like this one were first used as temporary shelters when Apaches moved about the countryside during raids. Today, many Apaches still prefer them to other types of homes.

although others still prefer to live in wickiups. Jerry lives in an adobe house with his father, mother, sister, and baby brother. They have electric lights and running water, but other Apache families do not have these things.

The Jicarilla have a tribal fund from the sale of the oil and gas discovered on their lands as well as a large lumber business. This money is used for all the people. Besides improving homes, they have built roads, schools, hospitals, a ski lodge, and a recreation center.

The Mescalero have no oil and gas on their lands. However, two government agencies, the Bureau of Indian Affairs and the Public Housing Administration, are arranging loans

Apaches who don't live in wickiups will often make their homes in a setting such as this.

for them so those who want to can improve their homes and install electricity and running water. They have a new community center with a council building, post office, barber shop, restaurant, dry-goods store, and grocery store. They have also developed a ski lodge and recreation areas into popular tourist attractions.

Jerry's family lives very much like their Anglo and Spanish neighbors in the Southwest. His mother buys her groceries at the supermarket and washes her clothes at the neighborhood laundry. Usually she wears cotton dresses in the latest fashion that she makes on her sewing machine. His sister Brenda also wears cotton dresses that her mother makes.

Just a few years ago, all Jicarilla children attended boarding school at Dulce. But now the Jicarilla have built new schools on the reservation. So Jerry and Brenda go by bus with other children to one of the new grade schools.

Mr. Vicente is a rancher, but sometimes he and other Apache ranchers work as firefighters. He has told Jerry how Mescalero Apaches were the first Indians to organize and train in fighting forest fires. They are known as the famous Red Hats.

Today, both the Jicarilla and Mescalero Apaches are carefully guarding their own forests from fire, because they want their wild deer, bear, elk, and turkeys to thrive. Aside from protecting the wild animals, the forests furnish both tribes with other sources of income, such as timber, which they sell in nearby towns or ship to other states.

With this added income, most Apaches who are ranchers and farmers are able to buy more food for their families than other New Mexico Indians. Their diet consists largely of beef, beans, potatoes, butter, and milk.

Like many Apache women, Jerry's mother keeps a dairy cow and grows a vegetable garden. Others buy their milk and vegetables from the supermarket.

Apaches govern themselves. Like the Navajos, they have a tribal council whose members are elected by the people. But their council functions under the rules of a charter and a constitution. Committees are formed to handle problems of education, housing, health, and welfare.

Chapter 9

IT IS GOOD
TO REMEMBER

Apache Religion and Customs

Jerry's grandfather is making a pair of deerskin moccasins for Brenda. He has rubbed the deerskin until it is as soft as rabbit ears. Jerry is helping him by rubbing and polishing four turquoise stones, which will be fastened to the moccasin laces. These sacred stones will bring good luck to Brenda when she wears the moccasins.

Mrs. Vicente and Jerry's aunt are also busy, hand-stitching a deerskin dress for Brenda and sewing fringes on the skirt and sleeves. Grandmother is gathering corn pollen to make yellow dye for the dress and moccasins. Using the yellow color will please White Painted Woman, the earth mother. After the dress is dyed, Mother and Aunt will paint it with symbols of such god beings as the sun, moon, morning star, rainbows, and clouds. When the dress is finished, Grandmother will sing songs over it so the spirits will be pleased and bless its owner.

Brenda will wear the dress and moccasins in the four-day coming-of-age ceremony that marks the beginning of womanhood. All Apache girls who are about twelve years

At their coming-of-age ceremony, Apache girls wear beautiful hand-made deerskin dresses, which are often embroidered with bead-work. Beadwork has become very popular among the Jicarilla Apaches, and has just about replaced the older craft of fine basket-making Apache women were known for. However, the two arts are connected in that Apache women now sew their beads in the same designs they once wove into their baskets.

old will take part. The ceremonial songs and dances give thanks to White Painted Woman (Earth Mother) who gave them her son, Water Child. Apaches believe that Water Child watches over them and drives away harmful evil spirits.

A few days before the ceremony begins, Apache men prepare the ceremonial grounds. They erect a large tepee in which the girls will be honored. Near the tepee, they build a long brush arbor where the girls' relatives may prepare food for everyone. A medicine man blesses the tepee, the girls, and their relatives.

During the four days, the special girls must drink only through reeds, and be careful that no water touches their bodies. They must not look at the sky for fear that rain will fall. They must not lose their tempers, speak harshly, or laugh loudly, lest their faces become wrinkled before they are old. If they obey these rules, they have proved their right to become young ladies, ready for courting.

Apache boys do not have a coming-of-age ceremony. However, when Jerry is twelve years old, he will enter the ceremonial races. The Apaches select a place on the open prairie for the races and set up their tents near by. In these races, the boys do not compete with one another to see who can run the fastest. Instead, both Apache men and boys run so their strength will return energy to "Life Giver," the Sun God. Apaches believe they must do this

Apaches gather for their ceremonial races to give energy to "Life Giver," the Sun God.

so that "Life Giver" will be able to make his daily journey across the sky and spread sunshine on all living things.

The runners paint their bodies in gray, brown, and yellow stripes and wear only breechcloths. One group races down the track, and another races back. They run as fast as they can, and the racing never stops. Old men stand on the sidelines urging the runners on. When a runner faints or falls with exhaustion, he is revived and sent back into the race. If a boy can last through the day, it is a great honor to his family. The races last for several days; during that time, Apaches live as they did in the old days. They cook on camp fires and sleep in the open.

They also perform a dance to the spirits who live inside their sacred mountains. Masked dancers representing the Mountain Spirits perform all night. There is always a clown, called The Grey One, who mimics the other dancers and entertains the children.

Apache songs and ceremonies have never been recorded, and many of them have been forgotten. But today, Apaches realize that their songs and dances are a part of their heritage and culture. As they try to recall as many as possible for their children, they write them down.

Apache songs are really prayers. They sing this song to guard against evil spirits:

Beautiful is the Mother Earth
Above her are the white clouds.
Under the clouds, the sun is shining.
In the warm sunshine,
Among the green herbs,
I walk where sunbeams are dancing.

Masked dancers representing the Mountain Spirits dance all night during the ceremonial races.

During the ceremonial races, Apaches live as they did in the old days. They set up tents and cook on camp fires.

Chapter 10

LEATHER BAGS AND WILLOW BASKETS

Apache Arts and Crafts

At one time, Apache women were excellent basket makers. But during their warring years, they stopped doing much of their handwork. Today some of the older women make baskets for ceremonies to hold their sacred cornmeal.

Sometimes Brenda goes with her mother and aunt to gather materials for making baskets. To make a beautiful basket, they will use different plants, herbs, and reeds. The spiny yucca plant is found on the prairie, the willow reeds along the creek banks, and the bark of juniper trees in the hills and in the mountains. To find these materials, the women travel in Mr. Vicente's pickup truck.

While Mother and Aunt gather reeds and bark, Brenda searches for plants and flowers to make dyes for painting the baskets. She looks for the blooms of rabbit brush to make yellow dye and Devil's Claw plant to make a shiny brown. She picks cactus blooms for red, rose, and lavendar shades.

Mother and Aunt plait the reeds to make open baskets of coil design. They form a small circle, and stitch rows of plaited reeds in widening circles around it. Some women

At an exhibition, an Apache woman weaves an ancient design into the ceremonial basket she is creating.

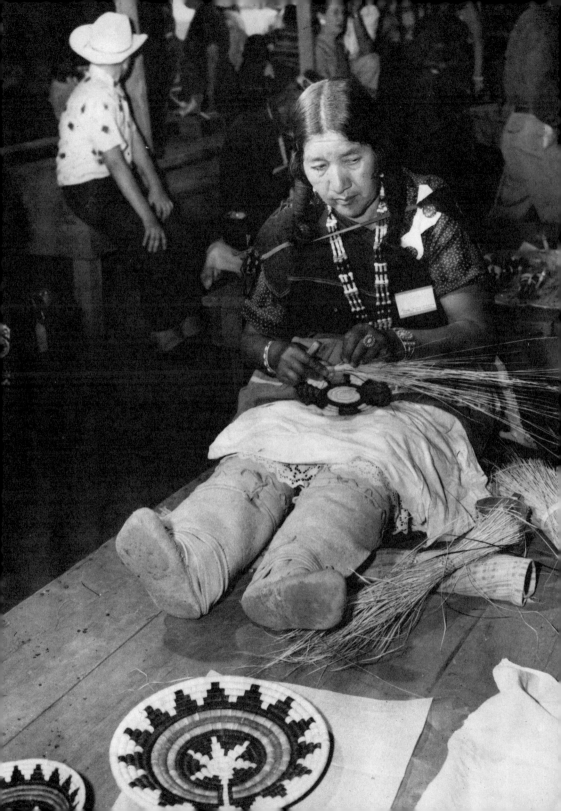

dye their reeds before making the baskets. Others paint designs on the baskets after they are made.

These baskets are both beautiful and practical. The flat ones can be used as trays or plates. Others are used as clothes baskets, flower vases, shopping bags, purses, and sewing baskets. Basket making is tiring work, and Apache women, like other Indian women, do not receive enough money for their handicraft.

Some Apache men are silversmiths and wood carvers. But Jerry wants to become an expert in leathercraft. Then he will make moccasins, belts, wallets, and purses. He is learning how to change deer and cowhides into soft leather. Grandfather shows him how to scrape the flesh and hair from the hides. When the hides are dried, they are very stiff, so the old man soaks them in water or buries them in wet sand before rubbing them with beef tallow.

Apache boys and girls are now learning these crafts in shops set up by their own people on the reservations. Members of their tribes are teaching them the ancient methods so they may carry on their beautiful art style.

OUR LAND GIVES US LIFE

The land is our mother, and from her comes life.
Life is the food we eat, the water we drink,
The earth we walk on, and the beauty we see.
To give this life, the land must be respected and
  cared for.
If it is exploited for greed and dollars, it will die.

The Navajos, as well as the Pueblos and Apaches, have always had a very close and special relationship to the land. However, since the arrival of the first white man, these Native Americans have had to struggle to keep this relationship alive and continuing.

Today's Navajos have heard tales of how their ancestors fought valiantly against white soldiers, who destroyed their crops and burned their homes. They have learned how the white man killed their ancestors, stole their land, and then put their people on a reservation. They know about the many broken treaties that have led to disputes over land rights, water rights, mineral rights, and timber and grazing rights.

But the bitter story of mistreatment by the white man is not over for the Navajos. Once again, their sacred religion and way of life are threatened.

This came about in 1964, when the Peabody Coal Company leased Black Mesa to fuel two of the six power plants they are building in the Southwest. Black Mesa, which is the Navajos' sacred Female Mountain, is also sacred land to the Hopi Indian tribe.

Now Black Mesa is being stripped. Strip mining starts on the outside and strips away all the trees, plants, and soil until it reaches the coal. Then the coal is scooped out, and the huge machines move on to tear apart another piece of land. At Black Mesa, the coal is then crushed, mixed with water, and forced through pipelines to supply the power plants.

The power plants produce electricity, but they also produce such pollutants as fly ash and sulfur dioxide, which settle over the mountains and reservation lands like a dark haze, and are very harmful to human, animal, and plant life.

Every day, a tremendous amount of water is used at Black Mesa. And Peabody is taking out the water in the worst way—they are tapping it from sources that cannot be refilled from the surface. The Native people are worried because they know that someday there isn't going to be any more water running out of the earth.

In addition, other companies want to run wires across Indian land to transmit the electricity from the power plants.

But how did all this happen?

Many Navajos feel they were tricked into giving the companies the right to run these lines across their lands. Some people were told to sign the paper giving consent, because they would be given free electricity. Others were told that the companies would be running only one small line, when they would actually be running two very large ones. Another lie told was that the Bureau of Indian Affairs and the Navajo Tribal Council had already approved the power lines, and it was just a formality to have the owners sign. Some people who signed later found out they would have to move, because the power line was to be run right through their homes.

However, the Navajos will not permit the white man to unjustly take any more from them. Like their ancestors, they are fighting back. Twelve Navajos have filed a lawsuit against the government and the companies responsible, to keep them from building any more lines. In this suit, the Navajos claim that they were not given all the facts about the project. They also claim

A Navajo newspaper said this about the destruction at Black Mesa:

"When the last of the coal is gone, the plants will stop, the money will stop, and then the land will be dead. The sun will be dim. The water will stink. When the grass is gone, will the People still know how to walk in beauty?"

that many of the people who gave their consent were made to sign forms written in English which were not translated into Navajo. Tribal Chairman Peter MacDonald has said that no power line is going to be built until everyone's grievance has been heard.

Many Navajos who want the mining stopped altogether have staged protest demonstrations at Black Mesa. These Navajos are not fighting over property. They are fighting to save the earth which gives them life and nourishes their soul. To destroy their holy land is to destroy their Earth Mother.

And the Children of the Sun will not allow this to happen.

INDEX

M

MacDonald, Peter, 90
Medicine man, 27, 38, 39, 59, 61, 62, 77
Mescalero Apaches, 70, 72, 73
Mexico/Mexicans, 10, 11
Monster Slayer, 58
Mother Earth, 27, 40, 77, 79-80, 90
Mountain Spirits, 79

N

Nabahe, Grandmother, 49, 51, 58, 63
Nabahe, Keedah John, 47.
  See also Keedah.
Nabahe, Mary Kay, 47.
  See also Ason-ne.
Nabahe, Mrs., 49-50, 51, 54, 63, 64
National Institute of Mental Health, 61
Native Americans, 9, 15, 17, 18, 56, 85
Navajos, arts and crafts of the, 63-69; daily life of the, 49-55; early history of, 9-10, 12-13; education of the, 56-57; government of the, 57; homes of the, 47-49; relationship to the land by, 85-90; religion of the, 58-62; tribal council of, 69, 87
New Mexico, 9, 11, 12, 13, 15, 17, 20, 23, 39, 46, 57, 70, 74

O

Obsidian, 39
Oklahoma, 15

P

Peabody Coal Company, 86
"People, The," 47
Plazas, 25
Pollutants, 86
Pottery, 40-43
Protestant, 34
Public Housing Administration, 72
Pueblo (village), 10, 43
Pueblo Indians, early history, 9-12, 64-65; arts and crafts of the, 39-45; customs, 27-32; education of the, 32-33; religious ceremonies, 34-38; villages of the, 22-27

R

Races, ceremonial, 77-79
Ramah High School, 57
Red Hats, 73
Religious ceremonies, 34-38, 58-62, 75-80
Reservations, 15, 17, 85; Apache, 70, 73, 84; Navajo, 13, 46, 54-57, 69; Pueblo, 12
Rio Grande, 23

S

San Ildefonso Indians, 43
Sand painting, Navajo, 60-61, 62
Santa Clara Indians, 24, 43
Santa Fe, New Mexico, 24, 31, 45
Santo Domingo Indians, 24, 43
Settlers, 10-12
Silversmiths, 40, 67, 84
Singers, 59-60
Snake Dance, 36
Songs, 38, 51, 59, 80
Southwest, 9, 10, 11, 34, 65, 73, 86
Spain/Spanish, 10, 24, 34, 39, 67, 70, 73
Spirits, 46, 49, 51, 59-61, 64, 77, 79
Strip mining, 86, 90
Sulfur dioxide, 86

T

"Tall girl," 47
Taos Indians, 24
Taos, New Mexico, 23
Tepee, 77
Tewa, 24
Texas, 11
Tiwa, 24
Towa, 24
Trading post, 54-55
Treaties, 12, 13-15, 85
Tribal councils, 18, 57, 74
Tribal government, 57
Turquoise, 39-40, 75

U

United States, 11, 12, 13, 15, 39, 46, 56, 57
United States Army, 13, 70
Utah, 13, 46

V

Vicente, Aunt, 75, 82
Vicente, Brenda, 73, 75, 82
Vicente, Grandfather, 75, 84
Vicente, Grandmother, 75
Vicente, Jerry (Geronimo), 70-77, 84
Vicente, Mr., 73, 75, 82
Vicente, Mrs., 73, 75, 82
Villages, Pueblo Indian, 22-23, 24, 25, 26

W

"Walk the Beautiful Way," 18, 36, 38
Washington, 13, 15
Water Child, 77
Weaving, 63-67
White Painted Woman, 75
Wickiups, 71, 72
Window Rock, Arizona, 57
World War II, 17

Z

Zuni Indians, 40